Keeping the Faith in
Interfaith Relationships

Series by the Messianic Jewish Theological Institute (MJTI):


*Messiah and Jewish Life Series*

*Messiah and Judaism Series*

*Messiah and Jewish Vision Series*

*Messiah and Christians Series*

*Messiah and Israel Series*

# Keeping the Faith in Interfaith Relationships

STUART DAUERMANN

WIPF & STOCK · Eugene, Oregon

Messianic Jewish Theological Institute
P.O. Box 54410
Los Angeles, CA 90054
www.mjti.com


Wipf & Stock
A Division of Wipf and Stock Publishers
199 W. 8th Ave., Suite 3
Eugene, OR 97401

www.wipfandstock.com

ISBN 13: 978-1-60608-446-5


Manufactured in the U.S.A.

"*SALAD, SOUP, and Goodies*" *is one of those big serve-yourself places where you can go grab seconds or thirds of a wide variety of foods. You can sit and eat all day if you feel like it. It's my favorite place to meet with people who want to talk.*

*This particular night I was waiting for Cindy, a beautiful Christian woman, and Jake, her Jewish boyfriend. Both came from large and loving families: hers, Los Angeles evangelicals and his, Reform Jews from Las Vegas.*

*The families loved Jake and Cindy, but Jesus, or Yeshua as we call him, had become an obstacle between Cindy and Jake, and a big issue for their families. Cindy felt she couldn't entertain the possibility of marriage unless Jake and she were of one mind on Yeshua, and Jake knew he couldn't and wouldn't make room in their marriage for Yeshua if it meant betraying his Jewishness and his family.*

*We met at the door of the restaurant as prearranged and, after getting full plates of salad and our beverages, made our way with our trays to a booth. After some small talk, we got to the reason they had asked to meet with me.*

## FIRST COURSE—THE SALAD

**Jake**    I think I could believe in Yeshua as the Messiah, but I have a problem.

**Stuart**    (I smiled.) I've heard that before, Jake. But everyone has a slightly different slant, and different issues. What are *yours?*

**Jake**    My Jewish identity and family are the most important things in my life. I love Cindy, and I want to marry her, and I think I understand why she's so adamant about her faith in Yeshua. Her mom and dad are the same way. But I can't, I won't, and I don't even want to think about believing in Yeshua if it means abandoning Jewish life and identity.

**Stuart**    (I mumbled through a mouthful of Veggie Won Ton Salad.) That all depends.

**Jake**    What did you say?

**Stuart**    (Swallowing a little more, I washed the mouthful down with Diet Pepsi and tried again.) That all depends.

**Jake**    Depends on what?

**Stuart**    (I looked at him and smiled.) That all depends on you!

**Jake**    What do you mean? (Jake was really tracking with me and returned my gaze.)

**Stuart**    It all depends on whether you want to keep living as a Jew. If you come to believe in Yeshua and abandon Jewish life, it will be your choice, nobody else's. If you want to treat believing in Yeshua like some sort of handy exit from Jewish life and community, go ahead. You can do that. Lots of people just like you have done it before, and lots of others are doing it all the time. But if you are the person of integrity I think you are, you won't do that. You wouldn't even think of doing that.

(He nodded, while I continued.)

Instead, you will treat belief in Yeshua as an entrance, a doorway into deeper Jewish loyalty and involvement.

**Cindy**    (Cindy and Jake both looked a little confused. Anxious about Jake, Cindy spoke up.) Can you tell Jake more about what you mean? To tell the truth, I'm not sure I understand myself.

**Stuart**  (I glanced longingly at the rest of my salad, but knew this was not a good time time to keep eating.) Cindy, you already know that Yeshua said, "I am the door."[1] The question is whether we see the door as marked "Entrance" or "Exit." The Bible is full of indications that Yeshua is meant to be the entrance into deeper Jewish involvement for Jewish people. But for two thousand years, too often he has been the exit. Yet it doesn't have to be that way. Jake, if you walk through the Yeshua door, the choice and responsibility will be yours as to whether you walk into or out of deeper engagement with Jewish life.

**Jake**  (Jake was stunned.) I never thought of it that way.

(He looked down and diddled with his salad a bit. As he looked up, I could see another question forming on his face. I also resumed my eating.)

I guess I could keep my Jewish connections and practices and let Cindy do her church thing, just so long as we agree to respect each other's choices.

**Stuart**  Tell me more. (I wanted to hear how Jake imagined things were going to work out between them. He went on.)

**Jake**  Believing in Jesus is important for Cindy, and I kind of wish I could believe like she does. I mean, it makes her so happy and resilient and all. In a way, it would sure make things simpler for us if we both believed the same way. And like we told you when we called you, being on two different sides of this fence means that we can't really get married, at least not yet.

But, let's face it, isn't believing in Jesus *really* kind of opposite to everything Jews believe? I could tolerate this for Cindy's sake, but I would need to keep these two compartments separate. I could let her have her religion and

1. John 10:9.

3

church-going, but I would have to keep my Jewishness alive and apart. And, Cindy, you would have to support me in that. Stuart, wouldn't this be the best way to handle things, so that everyone is respected and nobody is pressured?

Stuart  I suppose the two of you want to have kids. (They nodded.) Think about them for a minute. You know, children look to their mommies and daddies to tell them who they are. Am I right?

Cindy  Absolutely.

Stuart  So, if you follow this "two religions under one roof" idea, and your first child says to you, "Mommy! Daddy! What am I?" What do you say? "Well, Mommy is a Christian, and Daddy is a Jew, and when you grow up you can decide what you want to be?" Doesn't this sound a little like passing the buck?

Jake  What do you mean?

Stuart  I mean, the kid is looking to you two to tell him or her what he or she is, and you are saying, "Beats me! You'll have to figure that one out yourself when you get older!" How does that sit with you two?

Cindy  It's not good. And you're right: it's passing the buck. Our children need for us to be responsible, not to pass the responsibility back to them.

Stuart  (I turned my attention back to Jake.) Let me be a little bold here, Jake. I'll bet your Jewish practice up until now has amounted to seders, High Holy Days, Hanukkah lights, Purim parties, Bar Mitzvahs, funerals, weddings and checks to Jewish causes from time to time, right? A kind of "respectable minimalism?"

Jake  Yeah. (Jake blushed.) I guess you could say that.

**Stuart** Let me tell you in advance then, Jake. If you walk through the entrance marked Yeshua, you're going to find yourself called to go far beyond that. You'll be called to deeper Jewish commitment than you know now, and you will also encounter what the Bible calls the powers of the Age to Come. But it will be anything but "respectable minimalism." I promise you, it will be exciting, but it will be neither respectable, at least for some people, nor minimal. But that discussion will have to wait until later. First, let's go get some soup, and some bread to go with it!

**Jake** I'm right with you!

(Together, Cindy, Jake and I walked to the soup counter and grabbed some bowls, and after standing in line for a while, ladled out something hot, getting ready for a discussion that was sure to heat up, too.)

## SECOND COURSE—THE SOUP

(The soup wasn't bad. Cindy got clam chowder, Jake got chicken noodle, and I nursed a big bowl of potato leek.)

**Stuart** How about if I briefly outline the case for Yeshua being the entrance into a more abundant Jewish life rather than the exit.

(Their mouths were full of soup, so Cindy and Jake just nodded.)

Most of this is probably nothing new to you, but just for the record, here goes. First of all, Yeshua claimed to be the Messiah, and the New Testament of course makes that claim. In fact, "Christ" isn't his last name, it's just a Greek way of saying "Messiah." And if he claimed to be the Messiah, then you need to remember that the Messiah

5

wasn't just going to gather the Gentiles to the God of Israel, his first responsibility was for the Jewish people.

Jake  Wait. Slow down. The Messiah was supposed to gather the Gentiles to the God of Israel? Where do you get that?

Stuart  Isaiah says the Messiah would restore the tribes of Jacob, unifying the Jewish people, and also that he would be a light to the Gentiles.[2] Most Christian people remember the Gentile part and forget the Jewish part, and most Jewish people remember the tribes of Jacob part and forget the Gentile part.

Cindy  So what you're saying is the Messiah is supposed to unite Jews and Gentiles.

Stuart  I wouldn't say "unite," Cindy. I think the better word is "reconcile," what Paul calls "making peace." And he makes peace without forcing Jews to become Gentiles or Gentiles to become Jews.

Cindy  Okay. Yeah, I get it. This is getting interesting.

Jake  (Jake was getting frustrated.) Well, I don't think Christians think that way. I've been to Cindy's church a few times, and, they're nice people and all, but let's face it, everything about their Jesus is so, you know, *goyishe,* even if they do call him their Jewish Messiah. I think they would feel very comfortable if lots of Jewish people became Christians, as *goyishe* as they are. They don't seem to care a lot about Jews finding Jesus and holding on to Jewish life. For them, Jesus is the exit from Jewish life for Jews and the entrance into church life!

Stuart  Yeah, I know Jake. The Church has given Jesus a nose job, a new wardrobe, and a bleach job, so most Jews can no longer identify him as Jewish to the bone. And you're also right that most Christians don't really care if Jews in their

2. Isa 49:6.

6

churches stop living like Jews. But that doesn't change who he really is. And I think you can see that if Yeshua is the glory of God's people Israel, then we shouldn't treat him like some sort of exit from Jewish life, and no one should expect Jews who believe in him to assimilate into churchy lifestyles.

**Jake** Yeah, I get it, I get it. But it still doesn't hang together for me, not at all! From what I hear at Cindy's church, we don't have to keep the Jewish laws anymore. These people treat the Jewish way of life like it's expired or something. So where's the room for people like me to believe in Jesus and live like Jews? You can call Jesus the Jewish Messiah all you want, but if I lived like Cindy's church friends say we ought to live, treating the Torah like it's expired, well, you know as well as I do, I wouldn't be much of a Jew.

**Stuart** Well, Jake, Yeshua never intended it that way, and in fact, the prophets remind us that the Messiah strengthens Jewish life rather than destroying it. Ezekiel lived about 2600 years ago, and he said God would unify the Jewish people around the Messiah, and cause all Jews to keep the Torah.[3]

**Cindy** But isn't that just the Old Testament? I mean, isn't my church right that the New Testament teaches we don't have to keep the Law any more?

**Stuart** Not really, Cindy. I think you'll remember that Yeshua himself said "Don't think I have come to abolish the Torah and the Prophets! And anyone who annuls one of the least of these commandments and teaches others so will be called least in the Kingdom of Heaven."[4] That doesn't sound like the Torah is expired, does it?

3. Ezek 37:21–28.
4. Matt 5:17–20.

7

**Cindy** (Cindy was getting more upset.) Then why is so much teaching in my church about being free from the Law? You're confusing me! Are you saying my church is wrong?

**Stuart** Relax, Cindy. No one is attacking your church. Let's just say that many Christians are confused about these issues. Torah living was never given to the Gentiles. It was given as a guide to Jewish communal living. Nothing in the New Testament changes that: Jews are supposed to lead Jewish lives following Torah, while Gentiles are not called to the same obligations.

**Cindy** But can't Gentiles follow Torah if they want to?

**Stuart** I suppose so, Cindy. But if Gentiles really followed Torah, that would include the commandment for males to undergo ritual circumcision, and that makes them Jews!

**Cindy** But what about all that unity you were talking about a minute ago. It sounds to me like you are making a big division here. Aren't we all Abraham's children now that Jesus came?

**Stuart** You have a point, Cindy. Paul was clear: through faith in Jesus, Gentiles become part of Abraham's family.[5] But that doesn't mean they become Jews. That's why Gentiles don't have to keep all the commandments God gave to Israel. But it is different for Jewish Yeshua-believers. The Apostles and all the first century Jewish Yeshua believers understood that Torah was God's way of life for all Jews, including themselves. So yes, all of us who know Yeshua are Abraham's children, but only some of us are Jews.

**Cindy** (Cindy brightened.) Yeah. I like Jewish things and all. It would be a shame if Jews who believed in Jesus just threw all of that out the window! When I was a kid in Sunday school, I was always fascinated by how Jewish Jesus was.

5. Rom 4:9–16.

He kept the Passover, and he went to synagogue all the time, he went to the Temple. He did lots of Jewish things, but not just for show. It was just the way he lived.

**Stuart**   Are you surprised?

**Cindy**   Well, yes, I mean, no. No, really yes and no! I'm surprised at how Jewish the New Testament is, but I'm not surprised Jesus lived a Jewish life.

**Stuart**   Why not? Why aren't you surprised?

**Cindy**   Because he was a Jew!

**Stuart**   (I smiled.) That's it Cindy! That's the point! Jesus lived a Jewish life because he was a Jew. And Jewish people who believe in Jesus should live Jewish lives because they are Jews. And like I said, he didn't come to abolish the Torah and the Prophets. And certainly not to abolish Jewish life!

**Jake**   Well (Jake said, holding up his empty bowl), that calls for more food!

**Cindy**   (Cindy playfully punched Jake in his arm.) Jake! With you everything calls for more food!

**Jake**   (Jake laughed, pulling out of striking range.) What's the problem, Cindy? The place is called, "Salad, Soup, and Goodies." We had our salad, didn't we? And didn't we just finish our soup? Well then! It's time for goodies!

(We laughed our way toward the muffins, the soft ice cream, the gelatin deserts, and lots of other goodies. We each got coffee to bring back with us. Trying not to load our trays up too much, we made a U-turn back toward our booth. We still had some big issues to go over before Jake and Cindy would begin to comprehend what it means that Yeshua is the door into, and not out of, Jewish life.)

# THIRD COURSE—THE GOODIES

**Stuart**   (I thought that my discussion with Cindy and Jake had been going well. But since it always pays to make sure, I asked an open-ended question.)

So what do you think about what we've been saying tonight?

**Jake**   (Jake looked at Cindy as if to check out if what he was about to say would be all right with her.) Well, it all sounds pretty good, but I'm not convinced.

**Stuart**   Can you express the problem as a question, Jake? I'll try and answer, if I can.

**Jake**   Well, everything you're saying sounds pretty good, in fact too good.

**Stuart**   What do you mean, "too good"?

**Jake**   (Jake took a deep breath and looked me in the eye.) Your whole argument is too pat. I mean, if Christianity was as Jewish as you say, then how did Jesus become the exit from Jewish life, and how did Christianity get so, you know, other? It's not like this is a minority opinion or something. Everyone I have ever known, except maybe you and Cindy, and her family and all, thinks that believing in Jesus is the exit, really the end of Jewish life and community. And you keep talking about believing in Yeshua being so very Jewish, and how it's not the exit but the entrance. I don't get it. It all sounds like a scam.

**Stuart**   I don't blame you for being upset. A lot of people feel that way, and in fact I used to feel that way too. Let me see if I can at least begin to give an answer. Do we all agree that in the beginning, people understood that believing in Yeshua was a Jewish thing, and that it was right for Jews who believed in him to live as Jews?

Jake    Yeah.

Stuart  But things changed drastically. Keep following me now. Certainly by the second century and beyond, the Church began to be dominated by a Gentile majority. Gentile church leaders brought their Roman disdain for Jews and Judaism with them when they became Christians. Back then, Judaism was quite active in converting pagans, but so was the Church. As a competitive tactic, these Church leaders began denouncing Judaism, saying to the pagan world, "Why would you want to become a Jew? These people are cursed by God, they killed the Messiah whom God sent to them! Come join us instead! We are the new chosen people!"

Jake    (Jake turned a little pale.) That gives me the creeps. I knew a guy in school who thought that he was better than any Jew because he was a Christian. I didn't like him back then, and I don't like him now.

Stuart  I know how you feel, Jake, I've had those kinds of experiences, too. But you can see how this combination of a growing Gentile majority, and this distancing from the Jewish roots of Yeshua-faith led to Yeshua being an exit out of Jewish life and community.

Jake    I suppose so, yeah. (It was clear Jake needed more convincing.)

Stuart  But it got worse. The competition between the Church and the Synagogue continued for centuries. Not only were pagans attracted to Judaism, even some Christians were. Some Christian leaders, like St. John Chrysostom, preached vicious sermons against the Jews, as a means of discouraging his flock from attending Jewish services. By the sixth century, it was against state law in Christian countries for Jews to build synagogues, read the Bible in Hebrew, or even celebrate Passover before Christians celebrated Easter. Again, this was because of a sense of competition, and a desire to dominate the Jewish people.

Jake   Not exactly separation of church and state!

Cindy   Yes but didn't the government have anything to say about this?

Stuart   Yes, the government did. But that was part of the problem. In the fourth century the Emperor Constantine declared Christianity to be the official religion of the Roman Empire.

Cindy   I forgot about that. So the government was part of the problem.

Stuart   Yes it was. And with governmental pronouncements like the ones I mentioned, is it any wonder that Jesus has looked like an exit from Jewish life to Jews?

Cindy   Well, thank God it's not like that any more. But even if things are better now, why is it that Jesus *still* looks like an exit from Jewish life for Jewish people?

Stuart   Boy, that's a big one, Cindy. We could spend three days exploring that one. But I think we'd get thrown out of here before then! Let me take a few minutes.

I guess the first reason Yeshua looks like the exit from Jewish life is that there are a lot more Gentiles in the world than Jews, and any Jewish movement that opens its membership to Gentiles will eventually become mainly, even overwhelmingly, Gentile.

The second reason is that the Church said Jews who believe in Jesus are not Jews any more. By the second century, an idea began circulating that believers in Jesus were a third race . . . neither Jews, nor Gentiles. So, if you became a Jewish Yeshua believer, and were therefore not a Jew anymore according to the Church, why live like a Jew? The entire social context worked toward extinguishing Jewish identity.

That would be enough, but there are more reasons Yeshua looks like the exit from Jewish life.

**Cindy**   (Cindy smirked.) I can't wait.

**Stuart**   Well, let me give you some more examples, then.

You may remember, Cindy, that in the eleventh chapter of his Letter to the Romans, Paul warns the Gentile Christians in Rome not to be arrogant toward the Jewish people.[6] Well, the warning didn't take. By the second century, important leaders in the Church taught that the Jewish people had blown it, and that the Church was God's new chosen people.

**Jake**   (Jake winced). That sounds like God divorced Israel, and now the Church is his second wife.

**Stuart**   That's a painful comparison, Jake. But I think you are absolutely right.

**Cindy**   But I don't understand. In my church we learn that God has a special love for Israel. Didn't these people believe that too?

**Stuart**   Well, you need to remember that most of this was before the invention of the printing press, and the average person in your church knows the Bible much better than the Christians in those times. While it is true that some of their leaders were very knowledgeable in the Bible, still, their skewed attitudes caused them to miss some things and misinterpret others.

**Cindy**   What do you mean, "misinterpret"?

**Stuart**   Well, because they had already made up their minds that God had cursed and rejected the Jews, they either inter-

6. Rom 11:17–21.

preted the passages about God's unfailing love for Israel as if they were really about the Church, or they simply said the texts didn't apply any more because the Jews had committed the "crime" of rejecting Christ.

Jake   Lots of people still think that way. Let me ask you a question, Stuart. What would you say to someone who said that God had rejected the Jews because the Jews rejected Christ?

Stuart   I would tell them that Paul the Apostle says that God himself hardened the heart of Israel in order to bring salvation to the Gentiles.[7] God had a saving purpose in Israel's rejection of Christ, but this rejection is neither total or permanent.

Jake   What do you mean?

Stuart   Well, Paul says that it is only a portion of the Jewish people who have been hardened against believing in Jesus, and that there have always been some who believe in him like I do. And in one of those passages where Paul warns the Romans about arrogance, he reminds them that God's love for Israel is irrevocable.[8] Paul is clear that God is far from finished with the Jews. That's what I would tell the misguided Christian who thinks God is through with his people.

But most people have never dealt with these texts. So let me tell you something more about how far the Church has drifted from its Jewish moorings and how Jesus has become unrecognizable as the entrance to Jewish life.

Cindy   Please, go ahead. I've never heard these things before.

Stuart   This belief that the Jews rejected Christ, so God rejected them, and now the Church is the new Israel is called super-

7. Rom 11:7–11.
8. Rom 11:1–6, 28–29.

14

sessionism, or, replacement theology. It generally takes
three forms, each a little worse than the other. The puni-
tive variety says that because the Jewish people did not as a
whole embrace Yeshua as Messiah, God has rejected them.
They are no longer his chosen people, but the Church is.
We already discussed that one. Economic supersessionism argues that God has always intended Jewish religious
history to simply prepare the way for Jesus, and now that
he has come, the Jewish religious tradition has outlived
its usefulness. One famous New Testament scholar com-
pares the Jewish people to a postman delivering letters to
the Church.[9]

Cindy  Yuck!

Stuart  Closely related to this version, is something called struc-
tural supersessionism. Christians have learned to look
at the Bible as being all about personal salvation. In this
variety of supersessionism, the Jewish people as a distinct
people are not really necessary to the story of the Bible,
because the Bible is all about individuals, about getting saved, and about becoming part of the Church. The
Church decided that any Jews who became Christians had
to just get with the program, and forget about being Jews
any more. The Spanish Inquisition was all about this.

Jake  (Jake's face had become drawn and a little pale by now.)
What do you mean that the Inquisition was all about
this?

Stuart  The Inquisition was an inquiry. What was being inquired
about, under conditions of torture, was whether baptized
Jews were practicing Jewish life in secret. So, for example,
if there was no smoke coming out of the chimney of a

---

9. N. T. Wright, *What Saint Paul Really Said: Was Paul of Tarsus the Real
Founder of Christianity?* (Cincinnati, OH: Forward Movement Publications,
1997), 108.

baptized Jew on Friday night, the assumption was that the household was secretly keeping Shabbat. They were therefore subject to the cruel and torturous punishments of the Inquisition, and often, death.

Jake  After all you've said, what Jew in his right mind would ever want to believe in Jesus? In fact, what am I doing here? (Jake was livid. He had a right to be. He almost got up to go.)

Stuart  You make a good point, Jake. I used to think the way you do, and the way you are thinking is good and loyal to our people. There are only a couple of reasons why loyal Jews like you should consider Yeshua despite the mountain of hateful anti-Semitism we've been looking at.

Jake  (Jake paused before responding, his lips still tight with fury.) And what would those reasons be?

Stuart  They are what we could call the reasons of truth. First, all of us agree that this list of horrors doesn't describe the Yeshua of the Bible—they are not in accord with a book that itself warns against anti-Semitism, as when Paul reminded the Romans not to be arrogant. And it makes no sense to imagine that anti-Semitism is a right response to Yeshua, who taught that besides honoring God, the second greatest commandment is the commandment to love our neighbor. As a friend of mine said, "Do you believe that all these things happened *because* of the teachings of Jesus or *despite* the teachings of Jesus?" The answer is obvious. Christianity, which claimed to be the religion about Jesus, betrayed and utterly misrepresented the Jesus it claimed to represent.

Jake  Okay, okay. That's one of your reasons. What's the second?

Stuart  It's not only that Jesus didn't teach this way, but that his teaching and his claims demand to be heard because of the very weight of them. You can despise the Church Councils, and much of Church history, and the attitudes we have been discussing here. But despising Jesus is another thing. I think he at least deserves a hearing, don't you?

Jake   (Jake paused, looking down at the table. After about twenty seconds he looked up.) Yeah, I suppose so.

Stuart   A third reason is that the Bible teaches that Yeshua was sent into the world to die as an atonement for our sins. Now, whether you believe that or not is not the issue right now. What is the issue is that if the God of Israel sent Yeshua into the world to die for our sins, then, if you are serious about the God of Israel, it wouldn't be right to simply ignore what he had done. Does that make sense?

Jake   I guess so. But I'm not convinced about all that, you know.

Stuart   Yes, I know. But just theoretically, if he is the Jewish Messiah, then we have some decisions to make, right?

Jake   Okay. Right.

Stuart   (I paused myself before going on, taking a long sip of my now cold coffee.) But there's another reason you need to give a hearing to Yeshua, and it has to do with him being an entrance and not an exit.

Jake   What's the reason?

Stuart   You need to give a hearing to Yeshua because, if the Bible is true at all, God expects, no, requires you to go deeper into your Judaism than the respectable minimalism you are used to.

Jake   Do you mean I need to become an Orthodox Jew? Nobody in my family is Orthodox, although my mother's parents were real religious and kept kosher and all. Is that what you mean?

**Stuart**  I wouldn't put it that way, Jake. What I mean is that God has an agenda for the Jewish people, and if we as Jews are going to be serious about God and our Jewishness, we ought to at least sync our own agendas with his.

**Cindy**  (Cindy piped in, a bit anxiously.) But does Jesus have anything to do with this?

**Stuart**  Jesus has *everything* to do with this, because he plays a central role in that agenda. That agenda pops up all over the Bible, but I like the way it is summarized by the Prophet Ezekiel. In the thirty-seventh chapter of his book, he lists seven aspects of this agenda.[10] You'll find them very Jewish, and you'll find the Messiah precisely in the middle of them.

Here they are in the order Ezekiel names them: first, God is going to regather the Jewish people to the Land. At the very least, that means you should be a supporter of Israel, and an advocate for Aliyah.

**Cindy**  What's that?

**Jake**  Aliyah is moving to Israel. You know, like my cousin Sharon did two years ago. Remember?

**Cindy**  Oh yeah, I remember. I just didn't know the word.

**Stuart**  The second item on the agenda is Jewish unity. Ezekiel's prophecy says God will make the Jews one people in the land, *am echad.* We Jews need to remember that all Jews are our people. Despite whatever differences we might have, we are one very diverse family. And we should always do whatever we can to help other Jews and to preserve the bonds between us and them.

**Jake**  Yeah, but don't most Jews look at believing in Jesus as breaking that bond?

10. Ezek 37:21–28.

18

**Stuart** Good point, Jake. The answer is Yes and No. Many Jews do look at it that way, but when they see that Jews like my friends and I continue to live a Jewish life and to support the well-being of our people, they often come to see that we are not as they expected. They may not agree with us, but in many cases we win their respect and trust. What is important is not so much what you say as what you do.

**Jake** Hmm. It's like my Hebrew School teacher used to say, "Deed, not creed."

**Stuart** Something like that, although really, Judaism is a religion of deed *and* creed. The early Jewish believers in Yeshua agreed. Like Yeshua's brother, Ya'akov said in a letter he wrote, "faith without works is dead." That's just another way of saying creed without deed is dead.

My point is that all of us, if we are psychologically healthy, learn to make decisions that not everyone will agree with, even close-in people. Like you, Jake. When you dropped out of school to go into business, were your parents happy about it?

**Jake** (Smiling.) Not exactly thrilled.

**Stuart** But you did it anyway, didn't you?

**Jake** Yes, I did. Sometimes you just have to do things.

**Stuart** And why is that, Jake? Why did you feel you had to do what you did even though your parents disapproved?

**Jake** It was because I believed it was the right thing to do, and, well, I guess as you mature, you feel you have to be true to your own best instincts, otherwise you kind of stop growing, you know what I mean?

**Stuart** I know exactly what you mean. And it's the same thing with coming to faith in Yeshua as a Jew. When we make a decision like that, we should be well aware of how it will impact our family and friends, and that should matter to us. But when we do take that plunge, it's because we believe we must follow our own best instincts, and what we believe is right and true. And then, just like you in your decision to leave college and go into business, we must take care to succeed in our new venture.

Cindy  What do you mean by that?

Stuart  I mean that Jake will need to demonstrate that believing in Yeshua has made him a better Jew. Otherwise, it is like leaving college to go into business and ending up bankrupt. Not exactly what you wanted to do, huh Jake?

Jake  (Smiling again.) No, not exactly.

Stuart  And I can see by the Lexus you drove up in that you've been doing just fine in business.

Jake  Thank God.

Stuart  Well then, if you come to Yeshua-faith, you'll need to demonstrate a Lexus-level Jewish commitment, one that your parents will admire. And you'll need to do this not just to prove you were right in your decision, but because that is the way Jews are supposed to live. It's a matter of obedience. Yeshua wants our Jewish lives to be more abundant, not spiritually bankrupt, and that includes being observant Jews.

Jake  Interesting. You're really surprising me.

Stuart  How's that?

Jake  Well, when Cindy told me about you, that you were a Messianic Jew, I assumed, well, that you would . . . do you mind if I tell you something not exactly nice?

Stuart  Go ahead.

Jake  Well, I assumed that you would not be much of a Jew at all. I assumed you would be kind of like all the people in

Cindy's church, you know, Christian, but with a Jewish name and a Jewish face.

**Stuart** And?

**Jake** I've been learning tonight that you are really serious about being a Jew, that you look at Torah living as a requirement or something.

**Stuart** I prefer the term covenant faithfulness. All of us Jews are responsible to keep the covenant God made with our people at Sinai. Our people said, "We will obey and we will listen,"[11] and they were referring to being Torah observant. Every day I try and get a little better at obeying, listening to, and living Torah. Sometimes I don't do so well, but then I pick myself up and keep on keeping on. It's a way of life, and you just return to it when you wander away. Like our Torah service says, "all its ways are pleasantness and all its pathways peace." Torah living is a good way to live, and really, it's what God expects of us.

But let's get back to the list we were making of God's plans for our people.

(Cindy and Jake nodded, holding hands.)

We said that God's plans includes Aliyah and Jewish unity. The third thing he wants to do is to bring the Jewish people to spiritual renewal. Ezekiel put it this way: "I will give you a new heart and put a new spirit inside you; I will take the stony heart out of your flesh and give you a heart of flesh ... They will never again defile themselves with their idols, their detestable things, or any of their transgressions; but I will save them from all the places where they have been living and sinning; and I will cleanse them, so that they will be my people, and I will be their God."[12]

11. Exod 24:7.
12. Ezek 36:26; 37:23.

God is saying he is going to increase our people's *kavvanah*, our passionate focus on living as Jews. It won't be a matter of going through the motions, but instead, God will cause us to be passionate about our relationship with him and about obeying him.

Jake  "A heart of flesh instead of a heart of stone."

Stuart  Precisely. And the fourth item in God's plan is that he wants to gather us around the Messiah. Because this is the fourth item out of seven, it is the central item on God's blueprint for the Jewish people. Ezekiel puts it this way, "My servant David will be king over them, and all of them will have one shepherd."[13] When he speaks of David, he is speaking of the ultimate king in the line of David, and that is the Messiah.

Cindy  You mean Jesus, uh, Yeshua?

Stuart  Yes, we believe this is Yeshua, because we believe him to be the Messiah. And as you can see, he is right in the middle of a very Jewish agenda. He is not making Jews into Gentiles, but involved in the Jewish people returning to the Land, being united as a people, and being spiritually renewed.

Cindy  Wow. I never saw this before.

Stuart  No, I guess not. But this is a very Jewish Jesus, a very different Jesus than most Christians ever think about.

Jake  You can say that again! This would blow the doors off of Cindy's church.

Cindy  Jake! They're good people. They've just never thought about these things before. It would take getting used to, but these are people who love the Bible, and if the Bible

---

13. Ezek 37:24.

says these things, well, they would eventually come to terms with all of this.

Jake   Maybe, Cindy, maybe. But I don't expect them to really get this. After all, this is my world, and not theirs. These are not the kinds of concerns I expect Christians to have.

Stuart Let's continue, shall we? The fifth item on this list is that all Jews will return to covenant faithfulness, to living Jewish lives in obedience to Torah. That passage I quoted to you about the Jewish people gathered around the Son of David, the Messiah, has an interesting ending. Here is the whole verse: "My servant David will be king over them, and all of them will have one shepherd; they will live by my rulings and keep and observe my regulations."[14]

Jake   That's huge.

Stuart What do you mean? Why "huge"?

Jake   Well, it puts together everything you've been saying. The Messiah and Torah obedience, they're meant to go together.

Stuart And some day they will, Jake. That's one of the big things on God's wish list for Israel. Already more and more Jews are seeing the connection they never should have missed: that Torah obedience and faith in Yeshua the Messiah are not only compatible, but are linked together by God. And what it says in the Bible about marriage, also applies here, "What God has joined together, let no one separate."[15]

Cindy  This is very big, Stuart. If what you are saying is true, then, when Jake and I marry, and I hope we will, then I must do all I can to make sure ours is a Jewish home, and that I support him in his Jewish identity and responsibilities any way I can. Would that mean keeping kosher?

14. Ezek 37:24.
15. Matt 19:6.

**Stuart**  We're getting ahead of ourselves. Let's get the whole picture by finishing our list of seven things that God is up to among the Jewish people. We have seen that God is going to gather Jews back to our land, unify us as a people, renew us spiritually, bring us to honor our Messiah, and to obey God's statutes and ordinances—the particulars of Torah. Right?

**Cindy** and **Jake**  Right.

**Stuart**  The sixth item is that we will experience the relational reality of the Divine Presence, of what you refer to as the Holy Spirit, Cindy. Ezekiel says that God will make his home among the Jewish people, he will be their God, and they will be his people. This means that the kind of relationship God has always desired for the Jewish people will be at last fulfilled. We will enjoy and experience what holy people of all ages have only dreamed of.

**Jake**  May it happen soon!

**Stuart**  Absolutely, Jake. Soon and in our days. And that brings us to the final item: The Jewish people will be vindicated as God's people and he will be vindicated as their God, or as Ezekiel put it, "The nations will know that I am *ADONAI*, who sets Isra'el apart as holy, when my sanctuary is with them forever."[16] From the Bible's point of view, there is something out of joint about the Jewish people being scattered about, endangered in foreign lands, and harassed by their enemies. You know, the kind of thing you read in the newspaper every week. It not only makes the Jews look like they are not the chosen people anymore, it also makes God look powerless because he hasn't given his people a better life than this.

But in the end, everyone will know.

**Jake**  Know what?

16. Ezek 37:28.

**Stuart**   They will know that Israel is the chosen people, that God is able to deliver on his promises, and that Yeshua is the Messiah. Some day everyone will know.

**Cindy**   (Smiling.) But we know already, don't we?

**Stuart**   That's the way I see it, yes.

**Jake**   So where do we go from here?

**Stuart**   Well, I've given you both a lot to think about tonight, and the restaurant is about to close, so we've got to go. But there is much more we need to discuss. For example, we will need to look at what it might mean for the two of you to marry. What kinds of issues will you need to consider and work out together? These are big issues.

**Cindy**   (Soberly.) They sure are.

**Stuart**   Here's my suggestion. Why don't we meet again. You could come to my synagogue for a service and then stay afterward and we could talk.

**Cindy**   (Brightly.) That sounds like a great idea! (Looking at Jake.) Let's go, Honey! How about next week?

**Jake**   We have a Bar Mitzvah next week, remember? How about the following week?

**Stuart**   Shall we mark it down?

**Jake**   Yes. Let's do it.

**Stuart**   Sounds good to me! But for now, before they turn the lights out on us, let's go!

*Together we made our way to the front door. Because they had parked in the underground garage, and I on the street, we said our goodbyes just outside the restaurant door. It occurred to me that we had used the same door as an entrance as we did for an exit.*

*How appropriate.*

*Now we would have to see if Jake would walk through the Yeshua door to a more abundant Jewish life.*

www.ingramcontent.com/pod-product-compliance
Lightning Source LLC
Chambersburg PA
CBHW051051030426
42339CB00006B/308